discover ✦ countries

Poland

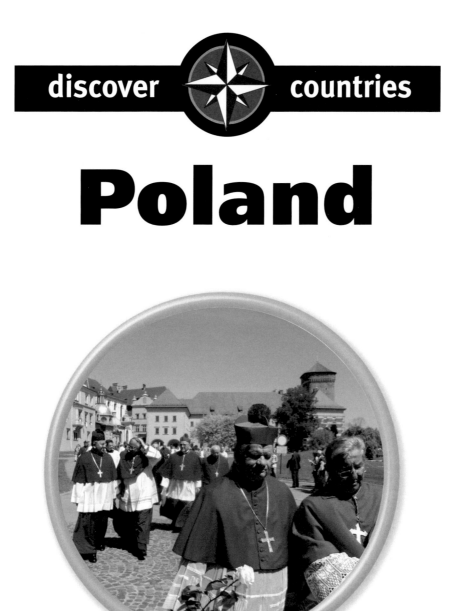

Rosie Wilson

WAYLAND

First published in 2009 by Wayland
Copyright © Wayland 2009

Wayland
Hachette Children's Books
338 Euston Road
London NW1 3BH

Wayland Australia
Level 17/207 Kent Street,
Sydney, NSW 2000

Editor: Paul Manning
Designer: Paul Manning
Consultant: Rob Bowden

Produced for Wayland by
White-Thomson Publishing Ltd

www.wtpub.co.uk
+44 (0)845 362 8240

British Library Cataloguing in Publication Data
Wilson, Rosie
Poland - (Discover countries)
1. Poland - Geography - Juvenile literature
I. Title
914.3'8

ISBN-13: 9780750257978

Printed in China
Wayland is a division of Hachette Children's Books
an Hachette UK company
www.hachette.co.uk

All data in this book was researched in late 2008
and has been collected from the latest sources available at that time.

Picture credits

t=top b=bottom l=left r=right

Front cover l, EASI-Images/Chris Fairclough; Front cover r, Shutterstock/Tatiana53; 1, Shutterstock/Tatiana53;
3t, 8, Shutterstock/Elena Grigorova; 3b, Shutterstock/Karol Kozlowski; 4 (map), Stefan Chabluk; 5, Wikipedia
Commons/Pko; 6, Shutterstock/Pawel Kielpinski; 7, Shutterstock/Pixelman; 9, Corbis/Andrzej Wiktor;
10, Shutterstock/Agata Dorobek ; 11, Shutterstock/Absolut; 12, Shutterstock/Dariush M.; 13, Corbis/Tomasz Gzell;
14, Shutterstock/Tatiana53; 15b, Shutterstock/Laurent Dambies; 15t, Shutterstock/Brasiliao; 16, Corbis/Andrzej Grygiel;
17, Corbis/Andrzej Grygiel; 18, Shutterstock/Puchan; 19, Corbis/Katarina Stoltz; 20, Jacek Bednarczyk; 21, Wikipedia
Commons/Joanna Karnat; 22, I-stock/Lukasz Kulicki; 23t, Wikipedia Commons/Piotrus; 23b, Corbis/Miroslaw Trembecki;
24, Shutterstock/Pixelman; 25, Shutterstock/Arway; 26, Corbis/Christophe Boisvieux; 27t, Shutterstock/Hamiza Bakirci;
27b, Wikipedia Commons/Cezary P; 28, Shutterstock/Martin D. Vonka; 29t, Shutterstock/Tomasz Otap; 29b,
Shutterstock/Photoaloja.

Contents

Discovering Poland

Poland is a country in central Europe. Slightly bigger than the UK, it has borders with Germany, the Czech Republic, Slovakia, Ukraine, Belarus, Lithuania and Kaliningrad Oblast (a small territory belonging to Russia). In the past Poland has been invaded or ruled by other countries, but it is now independent and has a democratic government.

East and West

Because of its location, Poland has always been a meeting point between east and west. Poland is mostly landlocked, but it has a coastline in the north. Its capital city, Warsaw, is located in the east, on the Vistula River. Poland is known for its fine churches, palaces and public buildings, and also for its troubled past – particularly during World War II, when millions of Jews were murdered on Polish soil.

The Communist era

After World War II, Poland became part of the Communist Bloc, a group

Poland Statistics

Area: 312,679 sq km (120,726 sq miles)

Capital city: Warsaw

Government type: Republic

Bordering countries: Belarus, Czech Republic, Germany, Lithuania, Russia, Slovakia, Ukraine

Currency: Zloty

Language: Polish 97.8%, Other 2.2%

of countries in central and eastern Europe under the control of the Soviet Union. For the next four decades, the country's economy belonged to the vast centralised Soviet system. In the early 1980s, Poland began to break free from Soviet control and to move towards democracy. In 1989, it became an independent democratic nation and the Republic of Poland was formed.

European Union

Poland joined the European Union in 2004. The EU is made up of 27 member countries which trade with one another and share important rights and freedoms. People in EU countries are allowed to travel freely in search of work, and member states have access to funds to help their economies to grow. Since Poland joined the EU, its economy has grown by 37 per cent.

Poland's future

As Poland trades more with other countries, its importance in the world is growing. But it also faces challenges. It is currently experiencing high levels of emigration as Polish workers leave the country in search of better-paid jobs in other EU countries.

DID YOU KNOW?
Poland's national flag was adopted in 1919. The white band at the top stands for peace. The red band symbolises the blood of Polish patriots who died in the fight for freedom and independence.

▶ Formerly the capital of Poland, Krakow is now a World Heritage Site and attracts seven million visitors annually.

Landscape and climate

Poland's landscape is mainly flat, and its green plains contain land that is good for growing crops. The country has a mild climate, with warm, wet summers and cooler, drier winters.

Borders

Poland's borders follow natural features. To the north, the Baltic Sea forms the coastal border. In the west, two main rivers, the Neisse and the Oder, divide Poland from Germany. In the south of the country, mountain ranges separate Poland from the Czech Republic and Slovakia.

Lowlands and lakes

Poland is low-lying, and three-quarters of the country is 650 m (2,133 ft) above sea level, or lower. Large river valleys run through the lowland plains. The main river, the Vistula, runs from north to south. Near the coast the Vistula spreads out into many channels to form a fan-shaped delta. South of the coastal area is a region containing over 3,000 lakes. Lake Sniardwy is the largest lake in Poland, and covers more than 100 sq km (38.6 sq miles).

Facts at a glance

Land area: 304,459 sq km (117,552 sq miles)

Area covered by water: 8,220 sq km (3,174 sq miles)

Highest point: Rysy, 2,499 m (8,199 ft)

Lowest point: near Raczki Elblaskie, −2 m (−6.6 ft)

Longest river: Vistula River 1,047 km (651 miles)

Coastline: 440 km (273 miles)

The Vistula, Poland's longest river, has been an important trade and transportation route since the Middle Ages.

Mountains

The Carpathian Mountains in the south of Poland are part of the same mountain range as the Alps. They stretch across the Czech Republic, Slovakia, Ukraine, Romania and Serbia in the south. Mostly covered with forest, they are home to some of the largest populations of brown bears, wolves, chamois and lynxes in Europe, as well as over one-third of all European plant species. In winter, heavy snow falls here – enough for skiing in some areas. The melted snow in spring is important for feeding Poland's rivers.

⬤ The Tatra Mountains, seen here in the distance, are part of the Carpathian range. They include some of the highest peaks in the country.

Climate

Poland's climate divides into six seasons. Early spring weather (March to May) varies from wintry to mild. Late spring (May to June) is sunny. A warm, rainy summer starts in July. Autumn in September is warm, then turns cool and damp in October. December brings a cold, snowy winter.

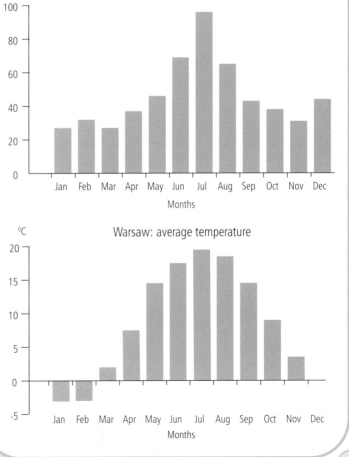

Warsaw: average rainfall
Rainfall (mm)

Warsaw: average temperature
°C

Population and health

Poland is home to 38.5 million people. Since 1960 the population grew by a third, but recently it has started falling. This is partly due to a drop in the birth rate, but also to emigration. By 2050, Poland's population is expected to fall by about 8 million.

A changing population

Historically, many different ethnic groups lived side by side in Poland. Before World War II, Poland contained large numbers of Jews, Germans and Ukrainians. By the end of the war, Poland's Jewish population had been almost totally wiped out by the Nazis.

Facts at a glance

Total population: 38.5 million

Life expectancy at birth: 75.4 years

Children dying before the age of five: 0.7%

Ethnic composition: Polish 96.7%, German 0.4%, Belarus 0.1%, Ukrainian 0.1%, Other 2.7%

▼ Emigration has significantly reduced the population of Polish cities such as Krakow.

During the Communist era, people were not allowed to move freely within the country, and travel to other countries was forbidden. Since the collapse of Communism, migration within former Communist Bloc countries has increased, and Poland's population has once again become more mixed. As Poles have left to find work abroad, immigrants have come to Poland from neighbouring countries, including Germany, Belarus and Ukraine.

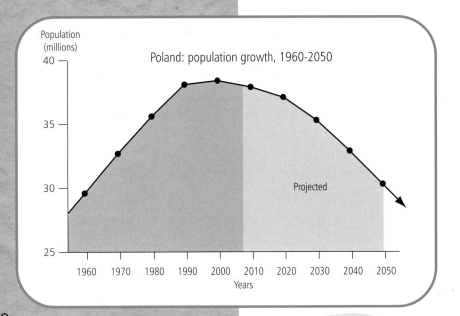

Poland: population growth, 1960-2050

Population (millions)

Years

Projected

Leaving Poland

Since 1995, people have been leaving Poland at a rate of more than 20,000 a year. Over the last four years, many young people have emigrated to other EU countries. In 2006 almost 50,000 left Poland: 18,000 to the UK and around 5,000 to the USA and Canada. Many more people leave Poland to work abroad and save money before returning home after a short time.

Health and diet

On average, Poles have lower life-expectancy than other Europeans, and the figure for Polish women is more than nine years higher than for men. Heart disease is a serious risk: the typical Polish diet is low in fruit and vegetables, and levels of alcohol consumption and smoking are high. Cancer is a major killer, and in 2002 around 45,000 Polish people died from different types of cancer.

DID YOU KNOW? Of all the countries affected by the Second World War, Poland lost the highest percentage of its citizens: more than six million died during the German occupation, half of them being Polish Jews.

Cancer screening at a clinic in Warsaw. Deaths from breast or cervical cancer in Poland are among the highest in Europe.

Settlements and living

Since 1950 the number of Polish people living in cities has steadily risen. In Poland today, 62 per cent of the population live in cities and urban areas. By 2050 the figure is expected to rise to 75 per cent.

Cities in Poland

The population of Warsaw, Poland's largest city, is about 1.7 million. Lodz and Krakow are the next largest, each with a population of around three-quarters of a million. Krakow is currently growing faster than Lodz because of the many international and Polish businesses located there.

DID YOU KNOW?

During the Second World War, 85 per cent of Warsaw was destroyed. Later many of the city's historic streets, buildings and churches were restored. In 1980 Warsaw's Old Town became a World Heritage Site.

The central square of Poznan in west-central Poland. Well-preserved medieval squares and market places are a feature of many Polish towns and cities.

Old and new housing

Much of the housing in Polish cities dates back to the 1950s. Many Poles live in large blocks of flats that were built quickly after the Second World War to house a rush of migrants from rural areas. Originally state owned, these flats are often cramped and poorly built. Since the 1990s more houses have been built. These are on the outskirts of cities and are privately owned.

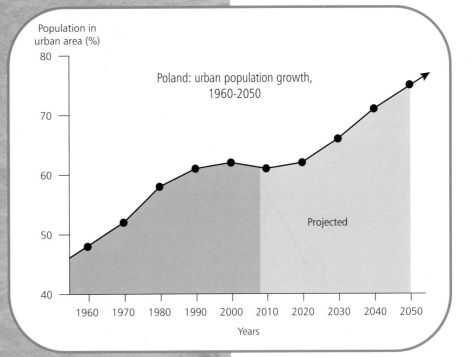

Rural Poland

At 38 per cent, Poland's rural population is higher than average for Europe. In the Polish countryside jobs are hard to find, and most emigration is from these areas. In 2006, 73 per cent of emigrants were from rural parts of Poland.

In the past, when people headed for the cities to find work, they would usually leave their families behind. Today, there is better housing available in urban areas, and whole families are moving from the country to start new lives in the city. This is helping to keep families together, but also speeding the depopulation of rural areas.

In the country, types of settlement vary. Some are small farming communities, with traditionally built, wooden and thatched houses. There are also larger settlements originally built for workers on Poland's rural estates.

⊙ Soviet-style apartment blocks dating back to the 1950s can still be found on the outskirts of most Polish cities.

Facts at a glance

Urban population: 62% (23.8 million)

Rural population: 38% (14.7 million)

Population of largest city: 1.7 million (Warsaw)

Population in urban area (%)

Poland: urban population growth, 1960-2050

Projected

Years

Family life

In Poland, family ties are strong and different generations of the same family often live close together. Traditionally, Poles like to stay in the place where they were born and grew up, but today many are finding they have to move away because of economic pressures and the need to find work.

Types of family

As a Catholic country, Poland places a high value on family life. Most couples marry, and many carry on living with their parents even after they are married so they can save money to buy a house of their own. Much of Polish social life revolves around the family. Even when both partners go out to work, parents, grandparents and children still meet for shared meals and leisure activities.

However, the age at which Polish people have children is getting higher – around 27 for women and 32 for men. Families are getting smaller, and many couples now have just one child. The divorce rate has doubled since 1970, and the number of couples who live together and have children without getting married is on the rise. Around 17 per cent of Polish households are now single-parent families.

⬘ Lifestyle changes and lack of affordable childcare mean that Polish couples are having fewer children.

The role of women

Under Communism, women were considered equal to men and were encouraged to go out to work. In the 1970s Polish women made up nearly half the workforce; many ran farms and small businesses, often earning more than their husbands.

In Poland today, many women have gone back to a more traditional role as homemakers and mothers. Government policy on issues affecting the family is also very conservative and reflects the strong influence of the Catholic Church. Abortion is illegal in Poland except for medical reasons, and there is no free contraception. One result is that levels of unwanted pregnancy are high among young people.

⊽ Polish Catholic women take part in an anti-abortion rally organised by the Polish League of Families (LPR).

Facts at a glance

Average children per childbearing woman:
1.3 children

Average household size:
2.9 people

Religion and beliefs

Although Poland is now a secular country, 90 per cent of Poles are Roman Catholics and a large number go to church regularly. Other religious communities include Eastern Orthodox (506,000), Jehovah's Witnesses (220,000), Protestants (159,000) and Jews (370,000). Since the 1970s Poland has also had a small but growing number of Muslim immigrants from Africa and the Middle East.

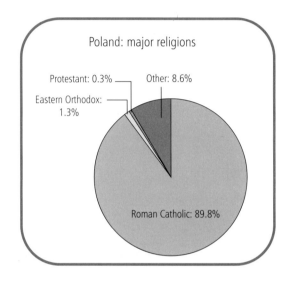

Poland: major religions

Protestant: 0.3%
Other: 8.6%
Eastern Orthodox: 1.3%
Roman Catholic: 89.8%

A Roman Catholic country

The Catholic Church has always been powerful in Poland and is involved in many different aspects of Polish life, influencing government policy on issues from education to abortion.

🔻 Catholic priests and cardinals gather to take part in a religious procession in Krakow.

Under Soviet Communism, the Catholic Church was seen as a symbol of national resistance to Russian occupation. This was strengthened in 1978 when the archbishop of Krakow, Karol Cardinal Wojtyla, was chosen as pope. During the years until his death in 2005, Pope John Paul II made several visits to his native Poland and became a powerful focus for opposition to the Communist regime.

Poland's Jews

The Nazi mass murder of Jews in the Second World War was one of the darkest chapters in Poland's history. Huge numbers of Jews from Poland and Germany were taken to the concentration camp at Auschwitz, where they were put to work in inhuman conditions or killed in specially built gas chambers. Poland now has several museums showing what happened to Jews during the war, and people from all over the world visit Auschwitz to learn about the Nazi Holocaust.

◐ Visitors to Auschwitz, where millions of Jews were murdered by the Nazis during the Second World War.

◐ A statue of Pope John Paul II outside the Holy Cross Church in Warsaw.

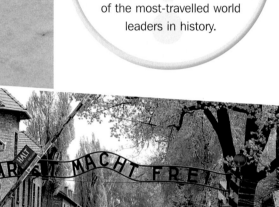

Religious customs

Christmas and Easter are important dates in Poland, and Polish people celebrate them in the traditional way with a family meal. Most Poles are named after Christian saints, and name-days are also marked with family meals, national holidays and gifts.

One pagan tradition that has survived is *Topienie Marzanny* or 'drowning the Marzanny', when children throw dolls that symbolise winter into the river. This is a celebration of spring, and takes place in March when the rivers are swollen with melted snow.

Education and learning

Learning has always been respected in Poland. Almost everyone in the country can read and write, and Poland's workforce is highly skilled. Because the country was isolated from the rest of the world under Communism, many skills that died out in other parts of Europe have been kept alive, such as traditional woodwork and building trades.

From school to university

Education for children in Poland is free, and children must go to school from the ages of 7 to 18. Most children attend nursery school (*przedszkole*) first. Next, they go to primary school and then two levels of secondary school, called *gimnazjum* and *liceum*.

Upper-level secondary schools offer vocational and technical training and prepare students for college. There are around 500 universities and schools of higher education in Poland, many of them privately funded. The four main universities each have a long history. The oldest, Jagiellonian University, was founded in 1364.

⊙ To celebrate the first day of the primary school year, these Polish schoolchildren receive bags filled with sweets from their parents.

⬤ Polish students sit an exam at a high school in Katowice.

Training for the workplace

Some Polish secondary schools teach technical skills, and Poles with a technical background can usually find work easily in other EU countries. Plumbing, electrical and other types of engineering are popular choices for Poles planning to work abroad. There are also colleges where people can learn farming, and schools offering courses in foreign languages including English, German and Russian, to help people find jobs overseas.

Sharing ideas

During the Cold War, it was often dangerous for Polish people to criticise the government publicly, so people joined church societies known as the Catholic Intellectual Clubs, where they could discuss issues without fear of arrest or imprisonment. Since 1989, censorship of the media has been lifted, and people can once again speak out and express their opinions freely. Newspapers, radio and news programmes on television are all popular, and the Internet is also becoming more important as a means of communication.

DID YOU KNOW? Under Poland's constitution, ethnic minorities are encouraged to speak their own native languages. Some ethnic groups have their own representative in the *Sejm*, the Polish parliament.

Employment and economy

After the collapse of Communism, Poland went through a difficult period as the country changed from a state-controlled system to a free market economy. Today it is the ninth-largest economy in the EU and the fastest-growing of all the former Communist Bloc countries.

Economic growth

Poland's first post-Communist government inherited many problems. In the late 1980s, it drew up a plan called 'Shock Therapy' to control inflation and to help people to start new businesses. After a slow start, Poland's economy started to grow. Since 2000, Poland's economy has more than doubled in size. After Poland joined the EU in 2004, it was able to trade more easily with EU countries. Because of the low cost of living in Poland, foreign companies could also pay less money to their Polish workers. This made it a popular country for firms to site their factories.

Facts at a glance

Contribution to GDP:
agriculture: 4%
industry: 31.6%
services: 64.4%

Labour force:
agriculture: 16.1%
industry: 29%
services: 54.9%

Female labour force:
6% of total

Unemployment rate:
12.8%

▼ The business district of the Polish capital, Warsaw.

Goods and services

Out of Poland's total workforce, 64 per cent now work in service industries. These are jobs such as nursing, teaching, banking, or working in shops and offices. A further 29 per cent work in manufacturing industries, making products to sell in Poland and abroad. Both men and women work in a range of jobs.

● Women workers at Inter Groclin Auto, Poland's leading car parts manufacturer.

Poland still has a higher proportion of agricultural workers than other European countries (16 per cent), but fewer today than in the past. Farms are more mechanised now, so fewer people are needed to work the land.

Unemployment

Even though the economy in Poland is growing, jobs are still hard to find, particularly in rural areas. In 2003, as many as 20 per cent of the workforce were unemployed, but this has now fallen to 12.8 per cent.

Because of the shortage of jobs at home, many Poles work abroad but help the Polish economy by sending money to their dependents. In 2007 Polish emigrants ploughed back roughly €6 billion into the Polish economy – 2.5 per cent of Poland's GDP. This money went mostly to support families and local businesses.

DID YOU KNOW?
In 1980 workers throughout Poland went on strike to demand better pay. Led by the Solidarity trade union, the strike eventually brought about the collapse of the Soviet-backed regime in Poland.

Economic growth (%)

Poland: economic growth, 1995-2006

Years

Industry and trade

During the Soviet era, most of Poland's trade was with other Communist Bloc countries, and contact with the outside world was restricted. Today the outdated factories of the Soviet era have been replaced with high-tech manufacturing plants, and Poland has a healthy import and export trade with other nations.

Goods for export

Under Communist rule, much of Polish industry was inefficient and uncompetitive. After 1989, output fell dramatically, but Polish industries soon started to become more efficient, and by the mid-1990s manufacturing was responsible for about 40 per cent of GDP.

With the help of foreign investment, Polish industry has continued to modernise and improve. Today, key exports include machinery and transport equipment, food products, metals and metal products, chemicals, beverages, tobacco, and textiles and clothing.

▶ Production workers at a truck and vehicle assembly plant at Niepolomice, near Krakow.

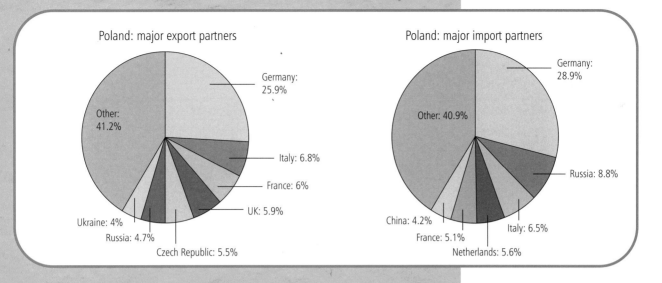

Poland: major export partners

- Germany: 25.9%
- Italy: 6.8%
- France: 6%
- UK: 5.9%
- Czech Republic: 5.5%
- Russia: 4.7%
- Ukraine: 4%
- Other: 41.2%

Poland: major import partners

- Germany: 28.9%
- Russia: 8.8%
- Italy: 6.5%
- Netherlands: 5.6%
- France: 5.1%
- China: 4.2%
- Other: 40.9%

Poland's natural resources

Poland has a rich supply of minerals and a history of mining that goes back to the thirteenth century. Today, mines extract coal and sulphur, as well as zinc, copper and silver. There are large coal reserves in the Upper Silesian region, and mining provides enough coal to supply the whole country's needs. Forestry is also important in Poland. Logs and sawn timber are exported as well as being made into products such as furniture, timber-frame buildings and paper.

Imports and exports

Poland's main export partners are Germany, Italy and France, but it also imports foreign goods, particularly machinery, chemicals and fuel. Almost all of Poland's petrol and petroleum-based products are imported, but a proportion of electricity generated in Poland – roughly 7 per cent – is exported. The bulk of the country's hydroelectricity comes from the Carpathians, the Sudeten region, and the Brda and Vistula Rivers.

DID YOU KNOW? The historic salt mine in Wieliczka, near Krakow, has been in continuous use since the thirteenth century. In 1978 it was among the first places to be named a UNESCO World Heritage site.

▼ A hydroelectric power plant at Zarnowiec, near Gdansk in northern Poland.

Farming and food

Fertile farmland is Poland's main natural resource, and agriculture is vital to the country's economy. There is much good-quality land, especially in the Polish lowlands and the Vistula River delta. Today Poland is one of the world's leading producers of rye and potatoes. Other principal crops include wheat and sugar beets.

Changing farms

Farming in Poland used to be organised through state farms. The government owned each farm, and there were enough farm workers to produce food for everyone in Poland as well as a surplus that was exported to other Communist Bloc countries. Most of these state farms closed after 1989. Today farms in Poland are privately

▼ Increasing mechanisation on Polish farms has reduced the need for agricultural workers.

owned and tend to produce for the export market, while Polish consumers eat cheaper imported food.

Crops and animals

Poland's main crops are rye and potatoes, but wheat, sugar beet and many varieties of fruit including apples and berries are also grown. Most farmers also keep livestock such as beef cattle, dairy cows, and pigs. The fishing industry in Poland is small, but sea fishing and fish farming still take place, as well as freshwater fishing in Poland's many lakes and rivers.

Food and diet

The traditional food of Poland is hearty, and includes lots of meat and potatoes. Beet soup (*barszcz*) is a traditional dish made from either red or white beetroot. People also eat mushroom soup (*zupa grzybowa*), as well as many different kinds of sausage. Cafés (called 'milk bars') that serve cheap but nourishing Polish food are still more popular than international fast food outlets. However, the large size of the portions and the lack of fresh fruit and vegetables in the typical Polish diet may be a reason why Poles suffer high rates of heart disease.

◔ Marigolds grown in the fields are harvested by a farm worker. The flowers are supplied to a range of industries and used to make creams, ointments and medicines.

DID YOU KNOW?
Cakes, biscuits and sweets are an essential part of any Polish feast. A special favourite is *nalesniki*, a traditional pancake served with fresh fruit, jam, or with a savoury filling.

◗ Soups and broths, often served with dumplings, are an important part of the Polish diet.

Transport and communications

By the time of independence in 1989, Poland's state-run transport networks were badly in need of renovation. Privatisation of the rail network began early in the twenty-first century, and soon other parts of the country's transport system were taken over, in whole or in part, by the private sector.

Getting around

Today Poland has high-speed railways and European-style motorways, as well as international airports at Warsaw, Krakow, Gdansk, Katowice, Poznan and Szczecin.

Approximately 20 per cent of Poles own a car, but public transport is also widely used. Warsaw now has modern, multi-lane highways, and other roads are being built to link the capital with other towns. However, many rural areas are still without good-quality tarmac roads.

Facts at a glance

Total roads: 423,997 km (263,460 miles)

Paved roads: 295,356 km (183,526 miles)

Railways: 23,072 km (14,336 miles)

Major airports: 123

Major ports: 4

▼ The Polish government has spent heavily to improve its road network. At present, three new motorways are being built to span the entire country.

Urban transport

In towns and cities public transport is cheap and reliable. Most people get around by bus, but trams and trolleybuses still run in many towns and cities. In Warsaw, a metro system opened in 1995. In 2007 it carried 300,000 people per day and is being extended all the time.

Waterways and shipping

Inland waterways are relatively little-used in Poland, with less than 1 per cent of Polish freight being carried on rivers and canals. However, shipping is well developed, and there are three large seaports, Szczecin (the largest), Gdynia and Gdansk, as well as many smaller fishing and coastal navigation ports.

Air travel

It is now possible to fly from Poland to 35 countries around the world. There are two main Polish airlines and many international airlines fly to and from Poland. Several flights a day run from the main airports in Krakow and Warsaw to Germany and the UK. Budget airlines also fly to Poland's cities, making Poland a popular destination for holidays and city breaks.

Global communications

Most households in Poland now have landlines, but mobiles are becoming more popular, with one for nearly every member of the population. Poles are also becoming more active Internet users, and many Polish families use Internet phone services, such as Skype, to keep in touch with relatives in other parts of the country or abroad.

● Warsaw's metro links the city centre to the densely populated southern suburbs. It is one of Europe's newest metros – and Poland's first.

DID YOU KNOW? Poland's rivers have a long history of navigation. The Vikings traveled up the Vistula and Oder in their long ships and in the Middle Ages the river was a key route for the transport of grain.

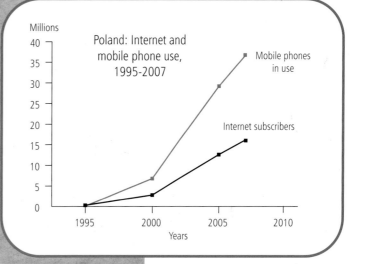

Poland: Internet and mobile phone use, 1995-2007

Millions

Mobile phones in use

Internet subscribers

Years

Leisure and tourism

With the growth of Poland's economy, people in Poland now have more leisure time and more money to spend on sport, cultural activities and travel. The abolition of state control of the media following the end of Communism has also added to the richness and vitality of Poland's cultural life.

Art and culture

Folk traditions including Polish music and dancing used to be encouraged under the Communist system, but are less popular than they used to be. However, folk music is still played at many weddings, and religious and national festivals are also celebrated with traditional music, dancing and costumes.

Over the years, many artists have kept the spirit of Polish nationalism alive through troubled times. Great names include the composers Frederic Chopin and Karol Szymanowski and the novelist Joseph Conrad, who wrote in English but remained a Polish patriot all his life. More recently writers such as Jerzy Kozinski (*The Painted Bird*, 1965)

Polish musicians and dancers wearing traditional costume in a market place in Krakow.

and film directors such as Krzysztof Kiezlowski (The 'Colours' Trilogy, 1993-4) and Roman Polanski (*The Pianist*, 2002) have raised Poland's reputation.

Sport and recreation

Team and spectator sports thrive in Poland. Football matches attract large crowds and most towns have good facilities for athletics (track and field) and swimming. Skiing and mountaineering in the Tatra Mountains and sailing on the Baltic or the Masurian Lakes are popular, and many Poles also enjoy cycling, horse riding, and *spelunking* (exploring caves).

Kite surfing on a frozen lake in north-central Poland.

Tourism

Cheaper and more frequent flights to and from other European countries have made a big difference to the Polish tourist industry. In 2005 tourism contributed about US$6 billion to the Polish economy, with most foreign tourists coming from Germany and the Czech Republic.

Cities such as Warsaw, Krakow and the site of the concentration camp at Auschwitz attract millions of foreign visitors each year. Poland's national parks are also much visited for their landscape and wildlife, which includes elk, European bison, wild boar and wolves.

The former salt mine at Wieliczka contains an underground chapel and scenes from the Bible carved by miners out of the rock.

Environment and wildlife

During the Soviet era, the environment and wildlife of Poland were badly damaged by industrial pollution. By the late twentieth century, Poland was one of the most polluted countries in the world. Today, the Polish government and the EU are trying to repair the damage and prevent further harm to the environment.

Industrial pollution

Many of the environmental problems that Poland faces today date back to the post-war period. In Upper Silesia and Krakow, factories produced some of the highest levels of air and water pollution in Europe. Several areas of central Poland where cement was produced and brown coal called lignite was burned also suffered serious air pollution.

DID YOU KNOW?
Poland is a key breeding ground for migratory birds. A quarter of all birds that visit Europe for the summer breed in Poland, particularly in the wetlands of the Biebrza, Narew and Warta Rivers.

▼ The stork is Poland's national bird and features in many Polish folk tales. The folk tradition of babies being delivered by storks originated in Poland.

Today Poland's major rivers are still badly polluted by industrial chemicals, and much higher than average levels of respiratory disease, abnormal pregnancies and infant mortality have been reported. Pollution has also reduced crop yields and stunted tree growth in many of the forests in the Sudetes and western Carpathians.

The effect on wildlife has been disastrous. Animals such as wolves and bears that once lived in forests have had their habitat destroyed and many species have been poisoned by drinking polluted water.

Making changes

Since the early 1990s, the Polish government has been taking steps to reduce pollution. Although the country still depends on coal-fired power stations, it has made its coal mines and coal production more efficient. More natural gas is being used to generate energy. Use of renewable energy sources is increasing. Hydroelectric power is growing, and Poland hopes to produce much more of its energy from renewable sources in future.

In the last few years, Poles have turned to biofuels to reduce carbon emissions. In towns and cities, more sustainable forms of transport such as trams and light rail systems are also giving people an alternative to travelling by car. The creation of large-scale national parks and nature reserves has also helped to create a safe home for many of Poland's endangered plants and animals.

◑ Once extinct in the wild, European bison have been been reintroduced in Poland's national parks.

Facts at a glance

Proportion of area protected: 11%

Biodiversity (known species): 2,984

Threatened species: 28

▶ A wind farm in Lisewo, northern Poland.

Glossary

abortion when a mother chooses to terminate a pregnancy

barszcz Polish word for beetroot soup, a favourite national dish

biofuel type of fuel produced from plants or plant-based materials

calorie intake way of measuring how much people eat. A calorie is a unit of food energy.

censorship when books, films or other forms of expression are banned or suppressed for political reasons

Cold War period of tension between the USA and the Soviet Union and their allies from late 1940s to 1990s

Communist Bloc group of countries controlled by Soviet Russia following the Second World War

concentration camp place where many people are imprisoned and/or forced to work in inhumane conditions

dependent someone who relies on another person, for example, for food or money

depopulation when people move away from an area and population decreases

export good or service sold to another country

extinction when a species dies out or ceases to exist

fertile good for growing crops

free-market economy system in which prices are governed by the laws of supply and demand

freight cargo carried by a ship, train or plane

GDP total value of goods and services produced by a country

Holocaust name given to the mass-murder of Jews by German Nazis during the Second World War

hydroelectricity energy generated by harnessing the power of water

import good or service bought from another country

inflation when the price of goods and services in a country is rising

liceum Polish name for secondary school

life expectancy average number of years people can expect to live

migration movement of people in search of work and better living conditions

mineral solid substance that is found in rocks or the ground. Salt, gold and limestone are examples of minerals.

natural resources water, soil, trees and minerals that are found naturally in an area

pollution poisoning or contaminating the environment with harmful chemicals

pope the leader of the Roman Catholic Church

privatisation selling a state-owned asset to the private sector

republic democratic country without a king or queen as head of state

rye type of cereal

secular non-religious. A secular country is one that does not have an official religion.

service industries part of the economy that provides services such as banking, retail, education and healthcare

surplus amount left over

thatch roof covering made of thick layers of straw

Topic web

Use this topic web to explore Polish themes
in different areas of your curriculum.

History
Auschwitz in Poland was one of the main camps where Jews were taken to be killed during the Second World War. This was known as the Holocaust. What can you find out about this?

Geography
In 2004, Poland joined the European Union. Find out what other countries were in the EU at this time. Can you locate these countries on a map? How many countries are in the EU today?

Science
Coal, copper, zinc and silver are all minerals that are found in Poland. Find out what you can about these minerals. Where are they found, and what are they used for?

Maths
The currency of Poland is the Zloty. Find out how many Zloty there are in £1. Choose some items (e.g. an apple, a can of cola) and work out how much they would cost you in Zloty.

Poland

English
Using the information in this book, write a story about a child your age who is Polish. Describe the scenery in the part of Poland where he or she lives.

Citizenship
Find out what life was like in Poland when the country was part of the Communist Bloc. Name three things that Polish people are allowed to do now that they could not do then.

Design and Technology
Using card or wood, make models of the brightly coloured houses on page 10 of this book. Paint your models and try to match the colours and patterns shown in the picture.

ICT
Imagine you are planning a holiday to Poland. Use the Internet to find out when is the best time to go and what are the main things to see.

Further information and index

Further reading

The Changing Face of Poland, Charles and Barbara Everett, (Wayland 2005)
Welcome to Poland, Umaima Mulla-Feroze and Paul Grajnert (Franklin Watts 2005)
Poland: New EU Countries and Citizens, Jan Kadziolka (Cherrytree 2005)

Websites

www.poland.pl
Information about Poland's culture and facts about the country.

www.cia.gov/library/publications/the-world-factbook/geos/pl.html
Key statistics about the landscape, population, economy, government, etc.

www.polishculture.co.uk
Information website run by the Polish Culture team for foreign nationals and Poles living abroad.

Index